HOPE FOR THE 22

The True Story of a Soldier Battling Despair and Suicide

LINO CAMACHO

Elani
PUBLISHING

Hope for the 22

Copyright © 2019 by Lino Camacho.

For information contact :
http://www.elanipublishing.com

Cover design by Peter Mitchell
ISBN: 978-0-578-58074-6

First Edition: September 2019

CONTENTS

DEDICATION

This book is dedicated to all those whom have served in the military of the United States and continue to serve this great nation. It is to bring awareness to the citizens of the United States of the horrible epidemic that has been plaguing veterans for years. It is to remember those who have lost their lives overseas and in country. Specifically, it is for those 22 veterans that have committed suicide every day for the past several years. My greatest mission in life is to save as many veterans' lives as I can through this book and the telling of my story. Most importantly, this book is dedicated to my wife, who has been by my side throughout the most difficult parts of my life, even when I was putting her through hell. I would also like to thank God who saved me from becoming one of the 22.

INTRODUCTION

I grew up with two siblings; one older and one younger, in a small town in California called, "Farmersville". Our parents were separated ever since we were infants, but our mother was always there for us. Our father was hardly around, and when he was, we were not sure what to expect. He would be a great father for a while but then suddenly he would become this loud, aggressive alcoholic.

He would come home with another woman's lipstick on his shirt, and physically and psychologically abuse our mother when we were too young to defend her. My mother would work as a waitress nonstop, so that she could provide for her three sons, since our father did not really take the role of provider for us. My father's mind was not only controlled by blind pride and arrogance, and the alcohol he consumed, but also the lustful thoughts that overwhelmed his mind. This turned him into a demonic person. We loved our father, and still do, but the love and affection that we did not receive as children created a void in our lives; which is why I began to find different ways of coping.

I began watching pornography at the age of six or seven, which destroyed my innocence as a child. The absence of my father's affection and love created an overwhelming addiction that lasted for more than 20 years. The only father-figure we had was my grandfather on my mother's side, who raised us with unconditional love and respect. We lived with our mother and our grandparents once we started going to elementary school. Our father lived in Mexico while we lived with our mother and grandparents in Farmersville, California. We always wanted to see our mother and father together because all we ever wanted was to see our mom and dad happy. Although our father mistreated our mother so many times, my mother still had the noble heart to teach us to love our father and forgive him continuously. If it was not for our wonderful mother, we would have grown up hating our father and disowning him completely.

God placed that forgiving heart in her, which is why my father still has children and grandchildren that love him dearly and will continue to pray for his salvation. It would have been nice to grow up with happily married parents who dedicated their lives to God, but everything happens for the better good of God's Kingdom. Through these experiences, God has made it possible for me to be able to connect with so many people around the globe who have grown up without a happy family, due to divorce, alcohol, unfaithfulness, pornography, and physical and psychological abuse, and so many other negative experiences.

I do not regret having gone through all these things because I know that God is going to use me as an instrument to bring hope to as many people as I can. I have come to realize that everyone has gone through traumatizing events that have shaped them during their childhood. I have met people that have shared their stories of rape, incest and eventually forgiveness through the Lord Jesus Christ and His saving grace.

When I was a child, I kept to myself and had a lot of anger built inside because of all the things that were happening to me. I would explode and become physically abusive with my brothers and other children. The only thing that would keep me calm when I was a child was when I would watch pornography, which is one of the reasons why I was alone a lot of the time as a child. There was no time for me to be a child because I would take every chance that I could to hide myself and watch pornographic images or videos.

And when I became a teenager, things grew even worse. I would avoid going out with my brothers, cousins, and friends because I would prefer to hide myself in a dark place and watch pornography because of the dopamine- the hormone would make me feel pleasure- that would be released while watching. I did not realize that pornography would only make me feel better for that moment, but eventually turn me into a lonely, perverted, and insecure teenager.

During all of the stress at home with my parents being divorced and my mom constantly trying to get back together with my father, I began puberty and acne began to grow all over my body and face. I would stress out so much because of the immense amount of acne I would have on my face, and warts that grew on my hands; it always felt as if I was never going to find a girlfriend because I felt so ugly. Then, my grandfather was diagnosed with cancer when I was around 13 or 14 years old, and I was devastated when I heard the news. I felt as if nothing in my life was going the way I wanted it to go. I wanted to be free of acne, warts, fighting parents, and sick family.

I am so thankful for an uncle that disciplined my brothers and I whenever we misbehaved because he helped us to learn how to treat our mother and grandparents with respect. Another person I am thankful for is my aunt Chacha who introduced us to a Christian church around this time because it made me feel like there was hope for my family and my life. Sadly, my grandfather died from the cancer. The disease had eaten his body from the inside out. He was always like a father to my brothers and I, which is why his death was so impactful in our lives. When I received the news, I was in Mexico with my father, and I remember feeling something like a knife puncturing my stomach. I felt so guilty for not going to see him because I had the opportunity to go and see him before he died, but I decided to stay with my father. A few months later, I witnessed my 18-month old cousin die from Leukemia in my uncle and aunt's arms, right in their living room. I remember watching my baby cousin bleed to death in their arms while hearing them cry out in agony. Although, both my grandfather and cousin died a horrific death due to cancer, I knew that they were in a beautiful place where there was no more pain.

As a teenager, I always knew that I would one day join the United States military because I wanted to be just like my grandfather, but I also joined because I wanted to save the lives of the helpless. I remember that I would pray for God to give me the opportunity to be able to save someone's life. I would pray for this even at around 11 years old. God works in mysterious ways because about a month away from graduation, my brother and I were helping my family move boxes to the front yard for a yard sale, and we heard a neighbor come out of her house yelling, "Dog attack, dog attack!" My brother and I dropped everything we had in our hands and began running towards the house. We jumped one fence after another, my brother even falling and getting stuck and causing me to laugh, but I kept moving towards the backyard, determined.

When I finally arrived, I saw a large dog attacking someone, but could not see clearly who it was. Without warning, I saw the dog grab a toddler with its teeth and toss the 18-month old infant into the air. As soon as I noticed that it was a toddler, I ran and somehow jumped, grabbed onto the roof and swung myself over a very tall chicken-wired fence and hit the dog in the back of its neck. As soon as the dog let go of the child, it tried to go after me, but I was able to get it into a headlock. Once I got the large dog in a headlock, another dog was trying to attack me, so I kicked it in the face really hard, and it ran off crying. While I was holding the dog in a headlock, I looked down at the little girl, and saw that she was full of blood, scratches and puncture wounds all over her head, face, arms, and legs. She looked pale blue and was breathing slowly. I thought that she was going to die because of how pale she looked, but I continued to pray while squeezing the dogs throat, and about 15 minutes later, the firefighters and the ambulance came and took the mauled baby away to the hospital.

Several days later, I was able to go see that same beautiful little girl walking and talking, as if nothing had happened. God gave me the opportunity to save that little angel's life.

THE JOURNEY BEGINS

I joined the Army as an infantryman with the intention of killing evil people around the world and saving the lives of the defenseless. However, I did not realize the sheer torture that I would have to go through in order to attain the title of infantryman.

It was a cold morning when I got to Georgia, and I remember getting on a bus headed towards Ft. Benning, where I was going to spend the next few months in hell. Everybody on the bus was quiet and had this look on their face that read, "What did I get myself into?" I had never been so nervous in all my life.

The bus finally went through the military checkpoint on the base and as we were closing in on the in-processing building on post, I saw eight drill sergeants with their round hats standing at parade rest just waiting for the bus to stop. As soon as the bus came to a complete stop, one of the drill sergeants ran into the bus and started getting into everybody's faces and cursing them out to force them off the bus as quickly as possible. The first smoking I had ever experienced was right off the bus in front of the in-processing building. When someone gets smoked in the military it means that you have to go through intense physical and psychological pain, due to long periods of exercise. It was going to be a long few months.

I remember experiencing a rude awakening when we got to the in-processing building because we were awake for three days straight without any kind of sleep, and it was the first time I ever hallucinated. The hallucinations occurred during some meetings inside a large classroom where we were signing documents half asleep. I remember seeing cars driving through the classroom while the drill instructor was talking. One pretty funny memory I have from in-processing was how some privates would fall over while standing at parade rest because of how tired they were. After a few months of training, lack of sleep, and smoking sessions, I was finally able to call myself an Infantryman in the United

States Army. It was one of the most exciting and proudest moments of my life!

Basic training was finally over, and I could not wait to go on leave. All I wanted to do is drink as much soda and eat as much junk food as I could. Junk food was considered contraband in basic training, so I was really craving it. Leave came to an end very quickly and I had orders to be stationed at Ft. Lewis, Washington near Seattle, when I got 2-2ID 1-17IN Bravo company, I had no idea what to expect, but I was already prepared to get smoked when I got there, which was smart because that is exactly what happened. I remember thinking to myself, "Ft. Lewis is such a beautiful place, but it is so depressing here." Washington state is probably one of the most amazing places I have ever lived in besides Texas.

Washington was the place where I met some of the most exceptional people in my life, my brothers-in-arms. Once I got to my company the 1st sergeant placed me into 1st platoon and the platoon sergeant assigned me to 1st squad as a SAW gunner. My squad leader was pretty intense, so he encouraged a 300 PT score or else we got smoked until we got stronger, so I only got below a 300 PT score once because I did not want to get smoked again. It was inevitable, however, as we got smoked for nearly everything because the platoon sergeant liked it that way. I do not regret it because he kept us on edge all the time, so we were never comfortable and were always ready for physical training tests.

It is so difficult to explain the relationship between the platoon sergeant and the guys in 1st platoon because he would let us know that we were the best in Bravo company when we would outperform the other platoons in PT, but then we would get smoked because not everyone would get a 300 PT score, the platoon sergeant included.

He was a scary looking dude, and no one wanted to get on his bad side. I remember when I accidentally ate his MRE's when we were training, and he started throwing MRE boxes all over the place, and I did not have the guts to say anything, so we just continued to listen to him curse us all out.

About two months after getting to my duty station, Bravo company went on a four-week training session in Yakima (YTC). I remember taking a ton of baby wipes with me because there were no showers out there. Yakima was a huge pain because we would go out on patrols throughout the day, and then again at night. I learned a lot of new things while training in Yakima; things like clearing a room, clearing a house with multiple rooms, flanking the enemy, squad formations, shooting methods, new methods of getting smoked, and how to patrol with night vision goggles on.

Training was something I loved and hated at the same time because of the hilarious and also frustrating moments that came with it. For example, there was a time when my team leader asked me why I had finished all of the ammunition so fast, and then started checking my ammo pouches and began to take out a ton of snacks out of my ammo pouches. I did not know what to say, but the only thing that came out was, "I was hungry." My team leader and squad leader had no other choice but to laugh hysterically while smoking me until they had enough. I remember laughing while getting smoked for the first five minutes, but then the pain set in, and it was no longer funny.

After coming back from Yakima, I started dating a girl. I really liked her, but unfortunately, it turned out that she was crazy. After I broke up with her, one of her friends sent me a message saying she had died in a car accident. Then, about two weeks later, she showed up in the barracks CQ and wanted to accuse me of stealing a blue truck and 5,000 dollars from her. My squad leader obviously had to investigate the situation, and went upstairs to check if I had any money hiding in my closet or in my bank account, but when he saw how much money I did have in my account, he started laughing hysterically because all I had was seven dollars to my name. He asked me what I spent my money on because I lived in the barracks, and I told him that I spent it on food.

After that incident, my squad leader told me to stay away from crazy women, and I tried my best, but that was not the case. I continued to look for the woman that was going to become my wife one day, but unfortunately, I found nothing but crazy after crazy along the way. But, one day I finally met someone whom I thought was going to become my wife. I fell in love with this woman and treated her like a queen and gave her everything she needed. A few months after meeting her, Bravo company received orders to deploy to Afghanistan. It was kind of a shock because I started worrying that I was not going to make it back. It felt like a dream when I received the news, but I was ready to give my life for my brothers and sisters and for this great nation.

This woman and I were making life plans for when I was to come back from Afghanistan. We were going to get married, have kids, travel, love one another and talked about being faithful to each other while away from one another. Finally, after eight

months of dating her, it was time for 1-17IN Battalion to deploy.

DEPLOYMENT

It was May 2012 and it was time to go overseas into Kandahar, Afghanistan for the 1-17IN Battalion, the "Buffaloes". Before getting to Afghanistan, we went through intense IED (improvised explosive device) training on an Airforce base somewhere near Afghanistan, so that we would be prepared for whatever circumstances we may face outside the wire. During the IED training, I remember thinking to myself, "What is not an IED out there?" It seemed as if everything was an indication of a possible IED.

For example, there were so many possible indications of IED's: ant trails, perfectly round objects, any kind of bottle or can, pens, people on cellphones, wires sticking out of a vehicle, cars that have a low rear, objects in the middle of the road, objects on the side of the road, rocks lined up, holes in walls, ceilings and ground. Every time I thought about the amount of possible IED's outside the wire, it made my stomach turn, which created this intense anxiety and fear that drained my energy. After a couple of weeks of intense IED training and rigorous weapon cleaning sessions, it was finally time for us to fly to Kandahar Airfield.

We got on a C130 and headed toward Afghanistan. Those seats were probably the most uncomfortable seats I have ever sat on, and we were seated for a while. It was not a very good experience, especially with a fractured tailbone. The C130 finally landed at KAF and the moment of truth had finally come, I remember seeing the ramp of that enormous plane slowly opening and feeling the hot breeze hitting my face. The air felt like opening the door of an oven. I was already sweating. It almost felt like I was dreaming when I saw the dry desert and Rocky Mountains all around, and at that moment I felt a twinge in my stomach and I remember saying to myself, "I'm here now, there's no going back."

As I was walking toward the building, I noticed bullet holes all over it, and there was a numbness in my fingers and all over my body. When we entered that building filled with bullet holes, we were briefed about many different responsibilities we had as a company, platoon, and as an individual. For example, a master sergeant spoke to us about the procedures after hearing the "incoming" sirens, or the sirens that meant there were bombs falling from the sky. A few days after getting to our tents, there was a really loud siren going off, and it sounded like the sirens in Texas when there is a tornado touching down. It scared me half to death. I remember seeing everybody jump out of their bunks with their weapons and headed toward the concrete bunkers outside.

I truly felt that I was going to get blown up, but I remember thinking to myself that at least I was not going to feel anything. I always prayed for my entire company to get back home alive, and I always asked God, "If anyone should die, let it be me." But that wasn't my only prayer. Every single day, I also prayed, "God, if I am about to die and I am going to Heaven, take me, but if I am about to die and am going to Hell, don't let me die!". This prayer, I believe, was the reason I came back alive.

Unfortunately, one day, my platoon sergeant received some horrible news about 2nd platoon. One of the NCO's had been blown up by an IED and he had lost both of his legs. When we heard about what had happened to him, we were in shock. I remember feeling this intense anger start to build in me. I still prayed for our buddies that had been hurt, but I was angry. The platoon was ready to go out and kill every single Taliban, and our platoon sergeant did everything he could to get us out on missions as soon as possible.

My platoon finally received instructions to leave the wire and go out on missions, but our platoon sergeant had asked us who was willing to stay an extra three to four weeks in order to get the MATV's ready for missions, and my squad leader and I decided to stay back. I wanted to stay back because I had the opportunity to call the woman whom was my fiancée at the time, and all I wanted to do is talk to her as much as I could because I thought that I was not going to come back home. It was really selfish of me to do, since my buddies were out there on missions and putting their lives on the line.

After several weeks of getting the vehicles ready for missions, my squad leader and I finally got on a chopper and headed to the strongpoint where our platoon was located, and it was even more nerve racking than when I heard the sirens going off. I knew it was time for me to put my training into practice, and this time I knew that if I screwed up on something it could be a matter of life or death.

Several guys from my platoon gave me so much trouble for staying back and not going out on missions with them for the next several weeks. They acted high and mighty because they went out on patrols before I did. It really ticked me off because I would pray for their safety every single day, during the weeks that I was not with them, and they would come over to me and call me a "POG". I did not let that get to me because I knew that one day, I would keep them alive. There were some buddies of mine that would even tell me that my fiancée was cheating on me with a bunch of different guys at the same time, and it obviously ticked me off, but I knew that they were just being jerks, so I tried to ignore them.

After a couple of weeks of wretched day and night shifts on the guard tower, I was on guard duty with one of my buddies one day and I remember hearing this snapping noise, and saying to my buddy, "Hey bro, I think we're getting shot at." My buddy told me that it was just some guy breaking wood below us, and I looked down and there was someone breaking wood beneath us. But I did notice some bullet holes in the guard tower that I never noticed before, but I tried not to think too much about it and continued to talk to my buddy. Shortly after we got off guard duty, we heard that there had been someone shooting at the guard tower, and I remember looking at him and not saying anything because our squad leader was right there, along with our platoon sergeant, who we would have gotten into a lot of trouble with if we said anything.

Bravo company finally received orders to be stationed on a COP in the Zhari province of Kandahar, Afghanistan; the birthplace of the Taliban. Our company got on several chinooks and flew into FOB Pasab, and from there we all took the MATV's and drove about 15 minutes to the COP and got situated into our designated areas. Once we were situated, two soldiers from each platoon were assigned to go on guard duty, and I was one of them. Every day felt like a hectic day. If you just got back from patrol, you had to either go on wall duty, guard duty, radio duty and cleaning your weapon was a norm during free time. Everyone was always doing something important, but there were also times when we got to relax and watch a movie, play video games, or talk on the phone with our families. We were definitely fortunate to have the opportunity to have some downtime.

After a few weeks on the COP, 1st platoon, my platoon, was sent to a strongpoint a few miles away from the COP. This was the lovely place where I was first introduced to burning everyone's poop. It was a pretty disgusting job, but at least nobody really bothered me. I actually preferred burning fecal matter over radio duty because I only had to worry about stirring the pot and putting more gasoline in, instead of worrying about getting all of the information written down on radio duty.

My platoon would take turns being on the COP and being on the strongpoint; I was attached to weapons squad and we would stay out on the strongpoint with 3rd squad for a couple of weeks and then switch with 1st and 2nd squad. The strongpoint was where we did not get to shower, or use any porter john, so the smell got pretty bad after a while. It was the best place, however, to create stronger relationships with my brothers-in-arms.

We slept near the ANA (Afghan National Army) and the ALP (Afghan Local Police) also known as the backstabbers, so I could not really sleep whenever it was time to sleep because I would wake up at every little sound, thinking that it was one of the ANA trying to kill me in my sleep. There was one time in the evening when the ANA rushed in the door while grabbing their weapons, so we all pointed our weapons at them. They said that there had been some trouble with the ALP and that they had threatened them. We were all pointing the weapons at the door with the IR lasers on, and all started to laugh. Someone joked, "Whoever comes in through that door is freaking screwed!" It was one of the funniest moments I had while in Afghanistan.

The first week I was on the strongpoint we went out on patrol by foot, and when we got about 250 meters away from the strongpoint, we began to hear shots fired from one of the guard towers. As soon as I heard the shots fired, I turned around and began to run towards the strongpoint. When we got closer, I could hear the snapping noise come above my head, so I knew that they were aiming at us. I finally got up on the guard tower and began to open fire on the Taliban about 300 meters to the west of the strongpoint. My buddies and I were shooting toward the Taliban and we could feel the rounds racing past our heads.

After that first firefight, it started becoming the new norm. We would go out on either foot patrol or mounted patrol and we would get shot at by the Taliban. There were several times when I thought that I was going to get shot in the head, but I always prayed that same prayer about not dying and going to hell. One day on the strongpoint, I had an unexplainable feeling that we were going to get shot at that night. I would constantly tell my buddies that I had a bad feeling about it. Evening had come and it was time for me to be on guard tower duty, so I was there for my shift. I told one of the other guys who was going to replace me to go back to sleep, so that I could cover their shift as well, because I felt that we were going to get into trouble that night.

I stayed on guard duty an extra four hours because of that bad feeling; and then it happened. My buddy and I were talking to each other when it got really quiet, even the crickets were silent. I told my buddy, "It got really quiet, all of a sudden," Just as I finished saying that, we saw about six tracer rounds coming towards us, which meant that there were about 25 to 35 rounds that came at us. As soon as the shots were fired, I got up on the window with my night vision goggles and my infra-red laser on and began to return fire. I instructed my buddies to turn on their goggles and IR lasers and shoot where I was pointing the laser. It was a really dark night, so we could only see the muzzle flash from the weapons, and they were only about 30 meters away from the strongpoint. Every single one of my brothers stood fast and continued to return fire, even as the bullets came toward them.

These were the true warriors that risked their lives to save every single one of their brothers. I truly felt that I was going to die because of how close the enemy got to our strongpoint. They were so close; definitely at grenade throwing distance from where we stood. I was praying during that entire firefight, and I thank God for allowing us to live that night because it was a miracle that we even came out of that firefight alive.

RECKLESS LIFE

After several months of restlessness, due to endless guard shifts, radio shifts, missions, patrols, and living with the sketchy Afghan local police, it was finally time for 1-17 Infantry division to go back home. It was the greatest news I have heard in a long time!

I was looking forward to going back home to my fiancée, so that we could start our life together as we had planned it. It was only after a couple of weeks of being back home that I found out that my fiancée was cheating on me for at least nine months, while I was deployed. The guy that she was cheating on me with sent me a message one morning and asked me if I was still going out with my fiancée. I obviously asked him who he was, and he let me know that he had been going out with her for the past nine months. We decided to meet at her house, so I waited for him in her living room. Shortly after speaking to the guy, my fiancée and I heard a knock at the door, and it was him standing there.

He began to explain to me everything that she had been

doing behind my back while lying to him that she was not dating me anymore. When I found out about her infidelity, I wanted to choke her to death. I was so angry! I hated the illusion she had created in my mind about starting a family, living together, getting married and so many other things. I began to break all her things that I had bought her, and then I took off driving fast. I finally came across this very high bridge where I was driving, and I was about to drive off the bridge to kill myself, but I felt something telling me to keep on driving because there was someone out there for me. I kept on driving to Ft. Lewis.

I was always faithful to the women I was with, until I got my heart broken by my ex-fiancé. I started to use that as an excuse to live my life as a womanizer and began to do some very disgusting things. I would go out with random women and have empty relationships with them. I would get drunk every weekend and my life felt so empty and without meaning for several months. Depression had become a normal part of my life and my mind was constantly thinking about buddies from basic training that had lost their lives. Along with my depression, I was also drinking my life away. The void in my life was being filled with alcohol and endless meaningless relationships with women who would cheat on me. I finally got to the point where I wanted to end my life. Back in my barracks' room, I got down on my knees and started crying and asked God to forgive me for all of the adultery I had committed. I asked God to please let the next woman I meet be my wife.

One day my buddies came into my room and asked me if I wanted to go to a nightclub. That was the last place I wanted to go, so I told them, "I don't want to meet any crazy chicks!", but they asked me if I wanted them to drive drunk. They guilted me into saying yes, so I went to be their designated driver. When we got into the nightclub, I had promised myself that I was not going to dance with anyone the entire night. I was the only weird guy dancing alone, until I got bored of watching everyone having fun dancing with someone and decided to look for a dance partner.

I began to look around for a decently dressed woman that I could dance with. I scanned the room until I finally came across this beautiful woman who was dancing with some friends. I stared at her until she looked at me, and gave her a little smile, but she looked shyly away. I continued to stare at her until she finally looked again, and I started dancing towards her. I got right next to her and asked her if she wanted to dance, but she said, "No thank you,".

I noticed she had a Hispanic accent, so that was when I asked her in Spanish and she looked surprised that, what appeared to be a white boy, spoke perfect Spanish. She ended up saying yes to the dance with me. I did not realize it then, but three days after praying for a future wife, I met the woman whom I was going to marry at, of all places, the nightclub.

Esmeralda was the most loving, kind, beautiful and amazing woman I had ever met. She came into my life at the perfect time because I had finally given up on searching for someone to marry. I was in a very dark place, and yet she made me happy.

HOMELESS

Four months after meeting Esmeralda I received my DD-214, and I was definitely excited to get out of the military. However, I had no idea how difficult transferring to the civilian life was going to be. I had a plan before getting out of the Army, but that plan was not a very effective one, because it was the only plan I had.

Shortly after I had gotten back from Afghanistan, I began the hiring process for Border Patrol Agent. It was a very long, expensive and annoying process. Before my contract was over, I was almost broke and I did not imagine how long it was going to be before taking the polygraph, which was the last step before getting into the academy.

There were multiple things I had to accomplish before getting to the polygraph: I had to pass the written exam, physical exam, and the interview. Two out of the three were very difficult. Furthermore, when I got out of the service, I did not want to live with my family because of the endless drama that went on, plus, some uncles were actually growing marijuana in my grandparents' backyard, and it was definitely going to impact my hiring process in a very negative way if I lived with them. I could not trust my mother because she took thousands of dollars out of my account while I was deployed, so I decided to stay away from everyone. So, I had no choice, I decided to live in my dilapidated old van until I received the polygraph appointment down in San Diego, California.

One of my uncles, who had been living in his car for about a year before I was homeless, gave me some really good tips like: attaining a gym membership so that I can shower there, and finding some good parking areas that do not tow you away. He also took me to go eat at some nice restaurants. He really helped me to not feel so lonely, which I am thankful for.

After a couple of months of living in my beat-up old van, Esmeralda found a family that she could live with as a nanny in San Diego, so she moved down from the state of Washington. It was, by far, the best news I had received in a while, since being homeless. I showed Esmeralda the van that I was living in for the past few months that we were apart. I tried to put some nice air fresheners in there. I was poor, but I at least wanted it to smell good.

Being homeless really sucked. I was living on $570 a month, and most of the money was either used for food, gas, or fixing the stupid van, so the money did not last too long. I would eat three bananas and three yogurts a day for three days out of the week. I was sometimes able to go out and have an awesome breakfast with

Esmeralda whenever she had a day off. Along with having a poor diet, I also suffered because there was no gas in my van for me to drive to the gym for showers. Sometimes I would go into the public restrooms in the parks and rinse off, using the sinks. It was very embarrassing for me because people would walk in and see me in my swimming shorts, lathering up with soap and walk out right away.

To top off the daily hell that I was living, this was all happening in the middle of Summer. I would constantly have to look for shade to park under because the heat was almost too much to bear, even with the shade. It probably didn't help that the windows in the van did not go down either.

During the day I would have to walk around different stores or plazas because of the extremely hot van. It really killed my feet because of the constant walking. In addition, walking around public areas really drained my energy because I was still constantly observing people to see if they had any possible explosives on them. At night, I would have to park my car somewhere that did not tow away vehicles in the evening. There would be nights that I would wake up thinking that someone was trying to break into the van, so I would pull out my knife and be ready to kill whoever was "breaking in". Not only was that an issue when I slept, but also when I would hear the fireworks go off in the middle of the night because of Sea World, which was close-by, I would wake up sweating, my blood pressure sky-rocketing, thinking that I was being shot at. I was also having some really crazy nightmares about firefights or people getting blown up, which would wake me up in the middle of the night because of how vivid the nightmares were.

Throughout the entire time living as a homeless man, I was applying for different jobs left and right and there were either no positions available or I was just denied employment. Every time I was denied a job, I would wonder if it was because all I had on my resume was being an infantryman. I felt like I was going insane.

The best times I had while being homeless were whenever I was with Esmeralda and my uncle, Enrique. They kept me sane through the hell I was living. I also had another uncle that was really supportive while I was homeless. He would call to check up on me, and sometimes I would receive a call from him at just the moment I started to think about buddies that lost their lives. My uncle Joe was also the one that encouraged me to apply for disability before getting out of the service, so I listened to him. A place I liked to go to a lot was the beach. Sometimes I would be there for hours until I would get tired of the heat or the sand. Five months after becoming a homeless man, I finally received an email with the location, time and date of the polygraph appointment. I was so excited because I could not wait to not be homeless anymore. Plus, I really wanted to be a border patrol agent. I wanted it because of the great pay and benefits that came with it.

I could not believe it! It was finally time to go and take the polygraph. Unfortunately, it was a three-hour drive north, due to traffic conditions. I also did not have much gas money. But I made it! As soon as I got to the office, I was received by this tall border patrol agent, and the first thing he said to me was, "If I catch you in a lie, I am going to automatically disqualify you, and you will never be able to join the border patrol, ever!". Once he said that I thought to myself, "Man, I won't be able to lie anymore!" I was all ready to lie about a few things.

The border patrol agent sat me down in this very uncomfortable chair about three feet away from the wall and began to place a ton of wires all over my body. When he was done connecting the wires all over me, he started asking me questions. One of the tough questions that came up was if I knew anyone who grew illegal drugs, and since I had to be honest, I told him that I did know someone, and they were my aunt and uncle. I noticed when I answered yes to that question, he started typing something in the computer, and then I thought to myself, "Ugh! I am screwed!" Four and a half hours later, he finally concluded the polygraph. He told me that he had passed me, but he had to send it higher up to see if they would pass me.

Now that I finished the polygraph, it was time for me to wait some more, and after another month of living in my van, I received an email with their decision. It read, "We disqualified you because you have an aunt and an uncle who grow marijuana," I was so heartbroken because this had been my dream job. After the sadness dissolved, I got really angry and started punching the van walls. I began to yell out some very stupid things against God and started blaming Him for all the hell that I was going through. However, once I calmed down, I began to think about all of the times that God had been there for me.

I remembered my time in Afghanistan and how I came out alive from those firefights, and how He brought back every single one of my buddies from my company alive. Then I remembered how He saved me from committing suicide on the bridge and other times when I was alone in my barracks room. I thought about that night that I prayed for God to allow the next woman I meet to be my wife, and three nights later I met Esmeralda in the place where I least wanted to go. After realizing all of the areas of my life where God intervened, I started asking God for forgiveness and decided to leave everything in His hands and put my trust in Him.

That same day I received the email about not qualifying for the position, I picked up my girlfriend, Esmeralda, and let her know the bad news. After hearing what had happened, she was so devastated because she knew exactly how much I wanted to become a border patrol agent. Esmeralda looked at me with a sad expression on her face, and while she was staring at me, I asked suddenly, "Do you want to go get married?". She said, "Yes." I was so surprised that she agreed to marry me. I was being denied left and right with multiple job applications and interviews, there was no money, no roof over my head, a garbage vehicle, and nothing to provide for Esmeralda, and here she was saying yes to becoming my wife.

A few days after she said yes, we went to the courthouse in San Diego and got married. It was an awesome day! Shortly after getting married, we decided to move up to central California where it was much cheaper to live and where my family was living, so we would have some kind of support.

LIFE WITHOUT PURPOSE

It was a new chapter in our lives and now I had to provide for both myself and my wife. I was so stressed because it was so difficult to find work and being a veteran with PTSD did not really help when it came to finding a job. I was fortunate enough to have an uncle who helped me get into the Ironworkers. I was able to find an apartment for my wife and myself. The pay with the Ironworkers was pretty good; however, it definitely had some drawbacks that came with it. I had to drive one-and-a-half hours to get to work and the workday consisted of 10 hours of nonstop lifting and walking in the scorching heat. It was a total of 13 hours I had to be away from my wife, and we had just gotten married. Plus, I would come home exhausted because of the trauma that I was putting my joints through. I was able to pay the bills, which was great, but I was not able to spend significant time with my wife. One day I got so sick and tired of being away from my wife that I decided to quit my job as an Ironworker.

I quit my job thinking that I was still going to receive another paycheck, so I figured that I would still have plenty of time to find another job before having to pay the next months' rent. However, I did not realize that they had already deposited my last paycheck. There was an incident a few weeks earlier on the job where I had smashed my index finger so hard that it swelled up and got bigger than my big toe. I went to the emergency room in order to avoid further damage. It was a couple of days after quitting my job that I received a bill in the mail from the hospital in the amount of $2,900. I stupidly decided to pay the whole amount, because I thought it would affect my credit in the long run, plus, I also thought that there was another paycheck on the way. Nonetheless, a few days after paying the large sum of money to the hospital, I finally noticed that there was no paycheck on the way because they had already paid me. This realization brought extreme anxiety to both my wife and myself, because we had to pay the rent in two weeks and there was only $350 saved up between the two of us.

There was nothing else we could do but pray, so we just prayed every day and every night. Until one day, I go to check the mail and received a packet that read Veterans Affairs on it. I realized then that it was the disability claim I had applied for several months back, and it said that I received an increase in my disability percentage, which backtracked to when I first applied for the disabilities. When I continued reading the award letter, I saw the amount of $5,600 that was going to be transferred over to my account on the first of the month. As soon as I saw how much we were going to receive, I started crying because we only had $350 saved up and the rent was due in a week. I showed my wife how much we were going to receive and then we both began to cry and to thank God for answering our prayers in a very timely manner. We could not believe how perfect the timing was to receive that amount just before the rent was due. We truly felt that it was a miracle.

Anxiety had finally ceased when it came to financial problems, but I still did not have the dream job I wanted, and I had no desire to look for another dead-end job. I still did not have control over my anger and worried about the people I would be surrounded by in any new job and how I would handle it. I just wanted to be alone. This was a huge issue for me and my wife because I started feeling like there was nothing else I wanted to do with my life when it came to a profession other than becoming a border patrol agent. Since I had no desire in finding a job or being around people, I wrongly thought that it was a good idea to start using the money to buy alcohol. I'd stay at home thinking about those who had lost their lives overseas and at home. However, staying home alone and buying alcohol was a very bad combination because it just caused me to spiral downward. Things became darker and darker for me.

It was the beginning of the path towards hell that I had just started to embark on, and neither my wife, nor myself knew exactly how dark the path was going to take me. Whatever PTSD symptoms I was having in the past, they only continued to get worse because I was adding alcohol into the mix.

My wife and I were saving up some money so that we could apply for her residency, since she did not have permission to work in the country yet. I was being a selfish idiot because I was too busy wasting the money on my drunkenness. The process kept on being postponed. My wife was getting tired of my stupidity and my drinking, so she decided to go and take care of one of our friends' baby, so that she would have some time away from me. Every time she was away from home, she felt relieved because she was not having to deal with my nonsense all day.

The problems at home were getting worse, and we were getting sick and tired of seeing each other. We would have some really big fights over something so small and insignificant. For example, my wife would supposedly give me a bad look, or my wife did not answer the way I thought she should, so then I would explode on her.

Throughout this entire time, I felt as if I was normal and that I did not have PTSD or anything else wrong with me, but I was completely wrong for thinking that way. Our arguments continued to get worse because we were always looking for a reason to fight, and we would fight about everything. If I did not do something right my wife would slam doors and yell, and whenever my wife would say anything that sounded like she was bossing me around I would yell at her and break things because I was the "macho man" of the house.

When the drinking increased, the fights would also increase, along with the intensity of the fights. For example, I would be drunk and then I would become physically aggressive with my wife. I would grab a hold of my wife's arms and squeeze them really hard and leave bruises on her.

The same uncle that helped me out when I was applying for disability and when I was homeless, would encourage me to drink with him almost every other day. I would go to his house and drink until I was completely drunk and then come back home. My wife would come home to a worthless, selfish, drunk who mistreated her. I was a monster and I am so thankful that my wife did not leave me because I was already planning to kill myself. I was falling further and further into the black pit of hell. My mind was so occupied with anxiety, stress, depression, hate, anger, and suicidal thoughts. It was one the darkest periods of my life because

I felt as if I had no purpose.

Not only was I messed up psychologically, but I was also gaining a ton of weight during this time. I had gained around 25 pounds since living in my van. There would be times when my wife would try to encourage me to go workout with her because I was getting so unhealthy, but I would automatically begin to question her motives and say, "You don't want to be with me when I am fat or what?" I was completely insane. My body was hurting, and I felt like I had the body of an unhealthy older person. I was having headaches, back aches, foot problems, ankle problems, breathing problems, as well as sleeping problems and so many other issues. Most of the physical and psychological problems I was having was due to the lack of adequate rest. I never had enough rest because I was always on edge and ready to defend myself and my family from any possible "threats", either during the day or in the middle of the night. There would be nights that I would stay awake for hours before I could go to sleep because of noises that came from outside the apartment.

The paranoia became a normal part of my life, along with other PTSD symptoms like depression, emptiness, anxiety, and suicidal thoughts. I had forgotten what it was like to be a sane person. Whenever my wife would try to hug me, kiss me, or tell me she loved me, I would just stay still and not respond. I was so disconnected from the world that I would not care about anybody's feelings. I had become so numb towards peoples' feelings, even my wife's, that I would not express any kind of affection towards her. It was tearing my wife's heart to pieces because I had become a completely different person than when we first met. When we were dating, I was always attentive, made her laugh, and made her feel loved. I stopped doing all of those things after we moved in together and definitely after I started drinking.

Not only did I suffer while I was awake, but I also suffered psychologically while sleeping because I would have nightmares that would wake me up, panicking because of how real the dreams were. Every time I would wake up from a nightmare, my heart would be pounding out of my chest and I would be sweating profusely because of how vivid the dreams were. Again, I was not the only one whom suffered, my wife would also wake up in the middle of the night because of the kicking and yelling that I would do while sleeping.

The nightmares I had were always bloody and dark. I would have dreams of body parts lying on the floor and blood splattered all over the floor and the walls. They were truly terrifying nightmares. I would also have dreams of demons chasing me in very dark places trying to kill me.

There was this dream that I had where I was staring at this really tall person that was covered in a black robe with a black and red mask on, standing in the middle of a dark room, All of a sudden the person pulled out his arm and it was nothing but bones and at the end of the fingers were claws, and he called me over to him. I began to walk towards him, and after every step I took towards, what I presumed was death, the room would get darker, until I finally started to think to myself that I was crazy for continuing, so I took a step back. As soon as I took that step back, the demon said something terrifying and wicked that I did not understand. When the demon spoke, I woke up right away because I heard this horrifying, demonic voice inside the room with me. I started looking around the room and I saw my wife staring at me, a terrified look on her face. I asked her if she heard that voice and she told me that the voice came out of me. As soon as my wife said that to me, all of the hairs on my body stood up because of how scared I was. I did not sleep for the rest of that night. I am sure nobody in their right mind would go to sleep after hearing that voice.

Throughout this entire time, I was living my life without purpose, and drinking my life away. Along with drinking, I was pushing every single person away from me, even my wife whom was the only one always there for me when I needed saving. I was digging my own grave while refusing my wife's help, and it continued to drag me deeper into the pit of hell. Several months of living this way had passed, and both my wife and I were so sick of seeing one another. We did not want to be together anymore and started planning to get a divorce. I got so sick of my wife one day that I told her to go back to Mexico. It was the darkest part of my life. I was continuously thinking about how and where to commit suicide. It was only a matter of time before going through with my plan. Thankfully, my wife did not give up that easily. She told me that we should start going to a Christian church just to see what happens with our marriage. I figured I had nothing more to lose, so I said yes.

HOPE FOR THE 22

The direction of my life's path changed as soon as I dropped my pride and determined that I needed help. Although it seemed as if there was no hope for me, the most crucial part of my life was the moment I decided to say yes to my wife's offer of attending church. My wife and I began to look up some local Christian churches in the area and we found one that caught our attention. We went in and the first thing I noticed was that there were a lot of elderly Caucasian folks, and we were the only young Hispanic couple. We did not go back to that church because we felt a little awkward being the only minorities there, so we continued to look for other Christian churches in the area.

Then we found this other church and decided to give it a try. Everything was going well for a while. We enjoyed the worship, the message, and the friendly people, but there was something that really threw me off. Towards the end of the service the pastor would ask people to raise their hands if they had any kind of pain in their bodies, so people would raise their hands and he would pray over them. I did not mind that, but what the pastor did after he finished praying for them was a little strange to me. As soon as he finished praying for them, he would ask them if they felt better and then put the microphone up to their lips, waiting until they responded. In other words, he was putting them on the spot in front of everyone, so my wife and I decided not to go back because we thought they were a little strange.

Although we could not find a good Christian church that met our expectations for a while, we did not give up. We finally came across this non-denominational Christian church called, Heart of the Valley. We decided to check out their services. We went in and met a lot of friendly people and felt like we were part of a family. When the worship music began, I started listening to the lyrics and I began to cry, I truly felt God's presence in that place. The feeling I had was indescribable. All of the emotions I was holding in for such a long time had finally come out and I was crying out to God for help. I no longer felt trapped. When the pastor finished preaching, he asked the congregation if anyone had any prayer requests they could come up to the altar and ask for prayer. I went up and asked them if they could pray for my marriage. After going to that first service at Heart of the Valley, we never missed a Sunday because we so desperately needed God in our lives.

We would attend church every Sunday and go to Bible studies every Wednesday to learn more about what it meant to be a Christian. The both of us grew up believing in God, but we never had a personal relationship with Him. We only prayed to God when we needed something or whenever there was an emergency. We were both raised Roman Catholic. My wife and I did not want to go to a Roman Catholic church anymore because we felt that it was more focused on rituals and traditions than having a personal relationship with God.

As a Roman Catholic, I never knew how important it was for everyone to accept Jesus as their Lord and Savior, until a Christian man told me that whenever we hear of Jesus and do not repent of our sins and accept Him as our Lord and Savior, then we do not receive salvation after death. In other words, if I was to die without accepting Jesus as my Savior after hearing from Him, I would burn in Hell for eternity because I willingly denied Him. After a few months of attending Heart of the Valley Christian Church, my wife and I decided to repent of our sins and accept Jesus Christ as our Lord and Savior and got baptized.

Once I was baptized, the suicidal thoughts that were controlling my mind disappeared because I finally decided to leave it all in God's hands. All the depressing thoughts that were continuously invading my mind had come to an end. God gave me a new mind and now I was free from the torture. It seemed as if someone just turned a light switch on, and all of the things that were torturing me were destroyed. The heads of those demons tormenting me were removed. The really bad fights we were having every day came to a halt as well. We both got serious when it came to trusting and living our lives for God and not for our own selfish ways. I knew that God was in our midst and that He was there to guide us through our marriage, and He was going to show us what our purpose in life was.

There was a drastic change when it came to having nightmares. Those bloody nightmares turned into spiritual dreams and visions. I began to have dreams of serpents trying to kill me every week. I realized that I was beginning to dream of serpents all of the time after getting baptized, so I decided to ask some people from church if they knew what the dreams might be trying to warn me about, and every single person I asked told me that the serpent represented Satan and that he was trying to kill me, but could not because as soon as I accepted Christ into my life he was not able to harm me anymore.

Although the devil could not drag me to Hell anymore, I was still going to have to fight against my own flesh, which meant that I was going to have to constantly fight against the things that I used to like. For example, I was going to have to stop doing all of the "fun" things that I would do in my past like getting drunk, cursing like a sailor, eating way too much, yelling at my wife, wanting to fight everyone that I did not like, watching pornography, and so many other things that I thought were fun.

In addition to having dreams of serpents after getting baptized, I also had this one dream that scared the life out of me because of how extremely real it felt. I woke up in my dream in the exact place where I had gone to sleep at and when I woke up in my dream I got up and walked to the restroom. As soon as I turned on the light and opened the door, I felt someone grab my arm really tight and pull me into the restroom. Whoever was trying to pull me in was trying to shut the door and lock me in, but I was fighting to keep the door open and struggling to keep myself from getting locked in. I looked up at the mirror and saw myself struggling to keep the door open and then I saw another person behind the door with an evil look on his face. When I looked closer it was half of my face staring back at me with a demonic look. I woke up right then, drenched with sweat.

I went to church and asked one of the pastors what the dream may be trying to say to me, and he explained to me that I was going to have to fight against my own desires in order to follow

God's desires in my life. I could honestly say that it really frustrated me to hear that, because I still wanted to hold on to some things I did in my past. I knew that he was right. I was having doubts about leaving my old life behind. The battle I was having against the demons went from being a fight without hope to a battle filled with hope because of the supernatural help from God. All those negative thoughts, feelings and emotions I was having of depression, death, hopelessness, loneliness, denial, betrayal, emptiness, anger, hatred, and suicide were eliminated because I gave it all to Jesus Christ.

I cannot keep myself from reiterating to my brothers-in-arms the importance of accepting Jesus as their Lord and Savior because He is the only One who could ever kill the void inside my soul, and give me a life filled with love, acceptance, holiness, hope, joy, and purpose. God saved me from the darkness and the hell that my life was. It is now my obligation to share the hope of life after death with the entire world, starting with the 22 veterans that need Him this day and the next and every other day after that. That Hope after death is Jesus Christ who gave His own life on the cross in our place so that we do not have to suffer the consequences of our sin, which is to burn in Hell for eternity. Religion teaches that people must work their way to Heaven, but Christianity is not a religion, it is a personal relationship with God and His Son.

Christianity is what God did for everyone to receive salvation because no one can receive salvation according to their own works. In order to be with God, everyone must be clean and free from sin. But nobody is clean from sin, that is why everyone needs Jesus in order to get to Heaven because He was the Ultimate Sacrifice, and now everyone can receive salvation by repenting of their sin and accepting Jesus as their Savior.

If it was not for me accepting God in my life, I would have become one of the 22 veterans who take their life every day. I am forever thankful to my God for what He has done to preserve and keep me. I hope and pray that every single veteran that reads this book can see the miracle that God can do in their lives if they only accept Him. My friends, it is time to drop the pride. It takes more strength to open up about issues in one's life than to stay quiet and deal with it alone.

I encourage every single person that is going through feelings loneliness, depression, sorrow, hopelessness, anxiety, sleeplessness, anger, betrayal, emptiness, and suicidal thoughts to seek help by going to a trained professional and talk about everything that is going on in their lives. I encourage you to speak to someone about your problems, but most importantly I encourage you to accept God into your lives so that you can see how much God will change your life for the better. God loves every living soul on this earth and that is why He gave His only Son as a sacrifice, so that everyone can receive salvation through believing in Him and repenting of their sins. I also believe that He has a purpose for everyone.

SOLDIER FOR CHRIST

Becoming a soldier in the United States Army has been one of the greatest titles I have ever achieved, and I know that the purpose I had as a soldier was to kill the enemy and protect those who were defenseless, but now God has given me a greater title and purpose, which is to kill the demons that continually torture and drag veterans into darkness. I proudly served as a soldier in the United States Army, and now I proudly serve as a soldier for Christ! As a soldier in the army, I always enjoyed singing while marching with my brothers and sisters, and now as a soldier in God's army, I sing a new cadence:

I'm sitting in the darkness, about to lose my mind; the devil tried to kill me, but I accepted Christ
Jesuuuuuuuuuuuuuuuuus (crush, crush, crush the devil's head!),
Saves souuuuuuuuuuuuuuuls (die, die, die Satan die!)
My buddy is in trouble, the devil's in his head; Jesus resurrected, He crushed the devil's head!

Jesuuuuuuuuuuuuuuuuus (crush, crush, crush the devil's head!),

Saves souuuuuuuuuuuuuuuls (die, die, die Satan die!)

I hear the angel's hovering, they're hovering overhead; they're

coming for the chosen, they're coming for the dead

Jesuuuuuuuuuuuuuuuuus (crush, crush, crush the devil's head!),

Saves souuuuuuuuuuuuuuuls (die, die, die Satan die!)

ABOUT THE AUTHOR

Lino Camacho joined the US Army as an infantryman and encountered multiple firefights while deployed to Afghanistan. He was a homeless veteran for six months after getting out of the military and later married his wife Esmeralda. They now reside in, North Texas, and they are pursuing their careers in education and occupational therapy. Now he is called to bring a story of encouragement and hope to those who are going through similar situations. Furthermore, Lino is focused on spreading the Gospel of Jesus Christ through his testimony, along with reducing the number of veterans that commit suicide in the United States.

Thanks for reading! Please add a short review on Amazon and let me know what you thought!

Made in the USA
Columbia, SC
29 January 2023

10657545R00038